The Ninth
International Congress of Orientalists

COMMUNICATIONS, PAPERS, &c.

Publishing Department:

ORIENTAL UNIVERSITY INSTITUTE

WOKING, ENGLAND.

INTRODUCTORY REMARKS TO AN INQUIRY INTO THE ETHNOGRAPHY OF AFGHANISTAN.

WHEN invited to become a member of this Ninth International Congress of Orientalists, and at the same time asked to contribute a Paper in furtherance of the work to be accomplished by the Congress, I gladly accepted the former proposal, because of the interest I have always taken in everything relating to the East; but with respect to the latter, though fully sensible of the honour thereby conferred, I felt some hesitation, owing to my inability to offer anything worthy the attention of the learned men who had devoted their lives to the acquirement of Oriental knowledge, and who would take part in the work of the Congress.

On reflection, however, it seemed to me that the present occasion offered a convenient opportunity to bring to the notice of learned Orientalists some results of a mass of miscellaneous information relating to the inhabitants of Afghanistan, which I had acquired during a long period of service in and about that frontier province of India; and more especially so as the course of political events in that quarter of Central Asia seems likely to bring the people of Afghanistan more prominently into notice amongst the Western nations than they have yet been by their previous wars with the British in India.

I decided, therefore, to prepare a Paper on the Ethnography of Afghanistan, as a contribution towards the work of the Ninth International Congress of Orientalists to be assembled in London in September, 1891, in response to the request above referred to. But, on looking over my

Paper for the **Ninth International Congress of Orientalists,**
London, September, 1891. Section (*f*).

1

notes and memoranda relating to the subject, I found they were so fragmentary and unconnected—jotted down as they had been at different times and on different occasions in odd intervals of leisure during the course of many years of varied official duties—that they could be utilized only as material in aid of an independent and methodical investigation of the ethnography of that region. As my memoranda and observations in this connection ranged over the wide area extending from Balkh-Turkistan to Balochistan in the one direction, and from the Indus Valley to the Persian Desert in the other, and thus covered the whole extent of the ancient Ariana, I thought I might venture to undertake an inquiry into the ethnography of that region under its modern name of Afghanistan, as comprehended in the extended application of that term.

On setting to work, however, I soon discovered that a bare enumeration of the various tribes and clans of the several distinct nationalities inhabiting that area,—without entering upon any detail of particulars relating to history, language, religion, manners, and physical characteristics,—was much more than could be intelligibly compressed into the limits of a paper to be read before the Congress. At the same time another difficulty presented itself in regard to the order in which the various and multitudinous array of tribes to be disposed of was to be dealt with. Under these circumstances it occurred to me that, considering the limited time for the work, the best plan would be to limit my task to a simple enumeration of the several tribes now found in Afghanistan, and to identify such of them as I could with the nations and tribes mentioned by ancient authorities as formerly inhabiting the region represented by that modern geographical term. Whilst with reference to the order in which they were to be dealt with, I thought it most convenient to take as my guide the earliest authentic record on the subject, and to prosecute the inquiry on the basis of the Persian satrapies described by Herodotus, "the Father of History;" and supplementing the information gathered from this source with that derivable from the works of the best-known of the later Greek and Roman writers, treating upon this part of Asia subsequent to its conquest by the Makedonians under Alexander the Great, as the groundwork of further investigation from more recent and contemporary sources of information, to put the whole together as briefly as possible.

This, in fact, is the course I have adopted, and with the result that, notwithstanding the limited time at my disposal, and my constant endeavour to be as concise as possible, consistently with intelligibility in the text, the inquiry has assumed the proportions of a small volume. This being the case, and fully sensible as I am of the many defects in my work, a doubt arose in my mind as to the propriety of submitting so hurriedly arranged and so imperfectly pursued an investigation to the criticism of the learned men who might take the trouble to read what I have written. But this doubt I at once set aside, under the conviction that the inquiry itself, however great its imperfections, presents the reader with at least a comprehensive view of the inhabitants of Afghanistan by their tribal nomenclature, such as has never before, so far as I am aware, been attempted, or at all events been accomplished, in the English language ; whilst at the same time it offers to the student of Ethnology the names of a number of very ancient and now obscure tribes, the investigation of whose history and antecedents furnishes a wide field for research of a most interesting, if not important, kind, in consequence of their ancient connection with the historical events or traditionary occurrences that took place in India on the one side and Assyria on the other, in ages remotely distant from our earliest authentic records.

Pursuing the inquiry after the manner above indicated, I have attempted no more than a simple statement of the names of the several nations recorded in history to have anciently inhabited this region to which our inquiry is limited ; coupling with them respectively their modern representatives by name, together with a list of the clans and principal sections into which each such tribe is now divided ; and noting such of these latter as I have, from independent personal observation and inquiry, recognised as representing ancient tribes on the sides of India, or of Persia, or of Assyria, as the case may be ; irrespective of such recognition having been either forestalled, or negatived, or unnoticed by others. In my explanations and affiliations of these tribal names I have doubtless made many mistakes, and for this reason am glad to think that my ventures in the direction indicated may lead others better qualified than myself to turn their attention to the subject and to give us the true identifications.

As above stated, this inquiry commences with the account given by Herodotus of the nations in his time inhabiting the ancient Persian Empire, of which the region engaging our attention constituted the eastern portion, and does not in any way treat of the nations which occupied this region at a more remote period, except incidentally when their posterity is re-cognised in the existing clans or tribes found at this day in various of the less accessible parts thereof. And even in this case as briefly as possible ; for to have described in any detail the many tribes now found in Afghanistan, whose names appear in the recitals of the Ràmayana and the Mahàbhàrat, or in the records of the Ràjatàringini, would have carried us away, however alluring the pursuit, far beyond the limits of the task I had undertaken at the outset of this inquiry. The subject is one of great interest, and awaits investigation at the hands of some Orientalist well acquainted with the ancient history of India, in respect to the relations of that country with Egypt and Assyria on the one hand and with Tartary and Tibet, including Burmah, on the other ; in which last quarter and Manipur, we find the namesakes of such tribes as the Khachin, Kùki, Khaki (Khakien of Burmah), etc., of the Indus border mountain ranges. For in the *Shloka* of the Ràmayana and the Mahàbhàrat, we have many important historical truths re-lating to the ancient colonization of the Indian continent by conquering invaders from each of the quarters above mentioned, all designedly concealed in the priestly phraseology of the Brahman, but with such exactitude of method, nicety of expression, and particularity of detail, as to render the whole capable of being transformed into a sober, intelligible, and probable history of the political revolutions that took place over the extent of India during ages antecedent to the records of authentic history, by any one who will take the trouble to read the Sanskrit aright through the veil of allegory so transparently covering it.

Of the several nations named by Herodotus and mentioned as inhabiting certain Persian satrapies, which were included within the area of the region afterwards known as Ariana, almost every one is at this day represented by a so-called Afghan tribe of precisely the same name, and in much the same situation too as that assigned by Herodotus to the ancient nation of which it is the relic or survival. The same may be said also in regard to the various nations mentioned by the later Greek and Roman writers as in their times,—the first two or three centuries of the Christian era,—inhabiting different parts of this region, which in their day had come to be known by a geographical nomenclature of provinces and districts unknown to Herodotus. But amongst the clans and sections of these existing tribes, bearing the names of the ancient nations above referred to, is found a variety of names evidently belonging to different races and nationalities the ethnic affinities of which afford an interesting subject for investigation.

Some of these clans and sections, especially all along the mountain ranges bordering upon the Indus, are at once recognisable by name as representatives of the posterity of nations of a remote antiquity in this part of Northern India and Central Asia, as recorded in Sanskrit writings, such as the Ràmayana, Mahàbhàrata, Harivansa, Vishnù Puràna, etc., and referable to aboriginal Indian races on the one hand and to early Skythic invaders, principally of the Nàga race, on the other. Whilst in other parts of the country, chiefly in Balochistan, are found tribes whose names indicate affinity with the ancient Assyrian and Babylonian races.

Besides these, there are other tribes, found in the areas of these ancient satrapies, and mentioned by Greek writers subsequently to the conquest by Alexander the Great, which bear names of a stamp different from the preceding, and clearly referable, some to Thrakian affinities, and others to Skythian. Amongst these last are classed, by the native Afghan genealogists, a number of tribes bearing Rajpùt names referable to the Sàkà Skythian races, of later arrival in India than the Nàga Skythians above mentioned, but earlier than the Jata Skythians who dispossessed the Greeks of Baktriana, and swarmed into India at about the same period that other Jata hordes of their kindred surged westward into Europe, as Jutes, Goths, and Vandals, the Jit, Jàt, and Mandan of our Indus valley tribes.

Coupled with these are certain other tribes whose names are found neither in the early Greek nor Sanskrit writings, but appear, some of them only, for the first time in Muhammadan authors of comparatively recent times, and, most of them, in the modern tribal nomenclature of the country. In this category are included representatives of the Alexandrian Greek conquerors, and later Turk and Mughal invaders, commonly designated Tatar; though the Tatar proper belongs to a much earlier period, being mentioned in the Mahàbhàrat as the Tittar, along with various tribes of Turk race.

The above brief sketch conveys some idea of the composite constitution of the existing population of the Afghanistan to which our inquiry is directed. The various race elements composing it afford so many subjects for special study and research, as to when and under what circumstances they came into the localities they now severally occupy in that country. In one or two instances I have ventured to indicate the origin of tribes whose true derivation was previously unknown and altogether unsuspected even by the very people themselves; although their persistent avowal of descent from a source different from that of any of the other peoples amongst whom they dwell, would have led one to expect the survival of some tribal tradition relating to their origin ; but if such formerly existed, as is very probably the case, it has long since been forgotten under the levelling influences of a jealous Muhammadanism, combined with the ignorance attending degradation and barbarism. So that now, though the knowledge of a dis-tinct racial origin survives, there is no legend, token, or tradition amongst the people to point out where the dis-tinction lies ; and in default of better information they are content to receive, certainly with more or less of indiffer-ence, if not incredulity as well, the silly fables concocted for them by Musalman priests as full of religious zeal as they are empty of historic lore.

The remarks just made in reference to some two or three particular tribes of Afghanistan may be appropriately ex-tended to most of the others of old date in the country, The absurd etymologies and stupid stories of the Musal-man genealogists in explanation of the names borne by various Pathan tribes have done much to obliterate the memory of traditions formerly current amongst the people. But, fortunately, proper names have seldom been distorted beyond recognition, in the case of the larger and better known tribes at least ; although, not unfrequently, some of the lesser clans have adopted purely Musalman surnames to the total effacement of the original patronymic ; even in these, however, the old name sometimes still lingers as an alternative appellation, or it is preserved as the ancient designation by neighbouring tribes. The tribal traditions, though largely corrupted under Musalman influences, for the most part retain some faint clue to, or hazy feature of, the original ; a lucky circumstance which sometimes enables the investigator to connect the garbled account with some corresponding record of authentic history.

For instance, there is the Baraki tribe of Kabul. This tribe is in Afghanistan acknowledged to be of different origin from all the other peoples amongst whom they dwell. But nobody mentions the existence of any tradition as to whence they originally came ; though themselves and their neighbour tribes with one accord declare that they were planted in their present seats in the Logar valley of Kabul by Mahmùd of Ghazni. But they say, with one accord also, that they are by descent neither Afghan nor Pathan, being excluded from their genealogies ; further, they say that they are neither Turk nor Tajik, nor Ghilzi nor Kurd, nor Hazàrah nor Mughal. In fact, of the Baraki tribal traditions really nothing is known for certain, and next to nothing of their peculiarities in respect to domestic manners and customs. They are known to use a peculiar dialect of their own amongst themselves, though ordinarily they speak the vernacular of the district in which they re-side ; those dwelling about Kabul using the Pukhto, and those in Kunduz and the Tajik States north of Hindu Kush using the Persian. Of their own Baraki dialect very little is known to others, and from the very meagre vocabularies of it which have hitherto been obtained no definite opinion can be formed, though it is probable that careful examination would disclose a great majority of Greek elements. The Baraki are a fine manly race, of generally fairer complexion than those amongst whom they live, and are sometimes quite as fair as Englishmen ; at least, I have seen two such. Amongst the Afghans they enjoy a reputation for intelligence and bravery superior to the ordinary standard of those qualities amongst their countrymen, and are credited with a loyalty to the ruling Barakzi dynasty so marked as to obtain record in the writings of contemporary native authors, and attested by their almost exclusive employment as the palace guards at Kabul since the time of the Amir Dost Muhammad Khan.

The Baraki possess their own hereditary lands, castles, and villages, and are principally engaged in agriculture and sheep-breeding, though many take service in the regular army, and some engage in trade as caravan merchants.

They are said to have formerly been a very numerous and powerful tribe, holding extensive territory throughout the country from Kunduz and Indarab, north of Hindu Kush, to the Logar valley and Butkhàk in the Kabul district, and to Kanigoram on the Suleman range; but now they are much reduced and scattered, their principal seats being in the Baraki castles of Logar, where they are agricultural, and in the Khinjàn and Baghlàn districts of Kunduz, where they are pastoral; they have lesser settlements in Kaoshan district on Hindu Kush, and in Kanigoram district on the Suleman range. They are reckoned at between twenty and thirty thousand families altogether, half the number being south of Hindu Kush and the rest to its north. In this latter direction their chief place is the village of Baraki in the Baglàn district of Kunduz; and this appears to have been the original settlement of the tribe in this part of the world. For it is said, as above noted, that they were planted in Logar by Mahmùd of Ghazni (in the beginning of the eleventh century), who afterwards gave them certain lands in Kanigoram as a reward for their services in his expeditions into Hindustan. As to the origin of the Baraki nothing is known by the Afghans; by some they are classed amongst the Tajik, and by others they are reckoned as Kurd; whilst the Baraki themselves prefer to be considered as Arab, perhaps of the Koresh tribe, that convenient refuge of so many of the wild tribes of these parts, who on entering the fold of the ennobling faith become ashamed of their poor relations, and willingly forget all about their early parentage. The foregoing is what we learn from the local sources of information available amongst the people themselves.

But from our more extended inquiry the Baraki of Afghanistan appear to be no other than the modern representatives of the captive Greeks who were transported, in the sixth century before Christ, by Darius Hystaspes, king of Persia, from the Libyan Bàrkè to the Baktrian territory, as recorded by Herodotus, who further tells us that the village which these exiles there built and called Bàrkè, was still inhabited in his time, which was about a century later.   It appears also from the passage I have quoted in this connection from Arrian, that in the time of Alexander's campaign in Baktria, say a century later again, the descendants of these Bàrkai, or Barkaians, were still there; and not only so, but also that their true origin was known to the followers of Alexander.   For although Arrian does not mention the Bàrkai by name, it can be only to them that he refers when incidentally mentioning the Kyrenes or Kyreneans in the passage above referred to.   For otherwise what could Kyreneans be doing in this distant part of Asia ?   If they were not the descendants of those who had been transported to this very tract by Darius from Barkè, a colony of Kyrene, then who were they ?   From the tenor of Arrian's account it would seem that these Barkai in Baktria were recognised as the posterity of the exiles from Kyrene, and that the history of their presence there was so well known at that time as not to require any special explanation in mentioning them by the name of the country whence they had originally come.   Besides, it is probable that in their passage of the Kàoshan Pass over Hindu Kush, at that time in the possession of these Kyreneans, as it is now of the Baraki, the Makedonian army received succours in the form of supplies and guides, which the historian, bent on magnifying the exploits of his hero, would not care to lay too much stress upon. The district in Baktria to which the Bàrkai of Herodotus were transported would appear to be the present Baghlan ; and the existing village of Baraki there probably marks the site of the village they there built and named Barkè. In the text of my " Inquiry into the Ethnography of Afghanistan," I have preferred, rightly or wrongly, the Baraki in Logar as the original settlement of the Bàrkai in these parts, because of its being the better known of the two ; though the Baraki in Bughlan accords best with the situation indicated by Herodotus—the district in Baktria—whilst the other is in Baktriana, or the wider territory of Baktria proper.

There was another body of Greek exiles recorded to have been settled, by Xerxes after his flight from Greece, in much the same part of this Baktrian country; namely, the Brankhidai of Milesia on the Hellespont. According to Arrian's account, their posterity settled in Sogdia, were exterminated, and their village there levelled with the ground and effaced altogether by Alexander, in punishment, it is alleged, of the crime committed by their grand-sires at Didymus. It is probable, however, that this punishment only involved the people of one particular village; many of their kinsmen residing elsewhere escaping the fury of Alexander. Anyhow it seems that traces of the posterity of these Brankhidai are still to be found in Afghanistan; where, indeed, formerly they seem to have been a numerous and widely-distributed tribe, to judge from the several different places bearing their name.

The original settlement of the Brankhidai, when trans-ported into Baktria, appears to have been in the modern Indarab district, north of Hindu Kush; where there still exists, in the hills to the east of Khost and bordering on Badakhshan territory, a canton called Barang or Farang, inhabited by a people called Barangi, and classed among the Tajik population. They may represent the ancient Brankhidai or Brankhoi, and perhaps in their original settle-ment in Baktria. There is another place not far distant referable to the same people, and situated to the west of Indarab, and on the south slope of Hindu Kush; namely, Barangàn, or Farangàn, a cluster of villages in the Ghor-band district; the name is the plural form of Barang, and a native of the place would be naturally called Barangi. A few miles from this place, is a very ancient lead mine, un-used for ages, and its existence apparently unknown to the people of the neighbourhood till its discovery by Dr. Lord in 1839-40; to judge from his description of it, the mine might well have been the work of Greeks, perhaps of the

Brankhoi, our Barangi, of the vicinity. The shaft, it is stated, descended one hundred feet perpendicular before it reached the ore; and the galleries had been run and the shafts sunk with a degree of skill that showed an acquaintance with the lie of the mineral, and an engineering knowledge that could scarcely be exceeded in the present day. Besides the above-mentioned, there is another district called Barang in the Nawagai division of Bajaur on the Indus border; probably so named after its former settlers, of whom traces might possibly be brought to light by local inquiry. There is also a village called Farangi in the Koh-dàman of Kabul, and another called Farangabad or Piringabad in the Mastung Valley, south of Quetta in Balochistan; both names are different pronunciations of Barangi, which is the same as the Greek Brankhoi, of which Brankhidai is a derivative. But besides these traces of Barangi occupancy, we have a clan of that name forming a division of the Syàni branch of the Lodi-Afghan, and comprising numerous sections as shown in our "Inquiry." The above-mentioned Baraki or *Bàrkai*, and Barangi or *Brankhoi* are both instances of Greek settlements in this remote frontier of ancient Persia at a period antecedent by several generations to the conquest by Alexander the Great. Inquiry would, no doubt, lead to the discovery of many other instances of Greek cities and colonies surviving to our day, and probably by names but little altered by the lapse of centuries, the changes of revolutions, and the succession of dynasties. In the modern town of Andikhoè, and the existing tribe of Shekh Ali, both within the area of the ancient Baktria proper; our "Inquiry," shows the one to represent the Antiokhia built as a Syrian city by Antiokhus the son of Seleukus; and the other to represent the Greek Aioloi, who, it would seem, colonized this part of the country in considerable strength, perhaps, as the chief or foremost tribe amongst those constituting the support of the Greek kings of Baktria. But these are by no means the only Greek names that our "Inquiry" has brought to notice, as will be seen by reference thereto.

The Alexandrian conquest of the Persian Empire no doubt brought about great and important changes in the population of the country. But it would appear that the Greek element had already become strongly diffused more or less throughout the wide extent of that sovereignty for centuries before the birth of Alexander the Great; and very likely this circumstance, in its way, contributed to the celerity and success of the military achievements of that great conqueror. Each of the four great divisions of the ancient Greeks—the Iònoi, the Aioloi, the Doroi, and the Boioi—had for nigh a thousand years prior to the Makedonian invasion, established powerful and flourishing colonies in Asia Minor, and these, in the pursuit of their own interests and affairs, were the means of bringing the sovereigns of Persia and Lesser Asia into more or less close relations, hostile or otherwise as the case might be, with the leaders of the ever unstable and turbulent Greek States in Europe. Further, it would seem that these Asiatic Greek colonies, at an early period after their establishment, sent out adventurous bands of emigrants, even into the far east of the Persian dominions. The Iònoi (Ionians), the Doroi (Dorians), especially, together with the Mysoi (Mysians), and Lydoi (Lydians), it would seem, advanced eastwards up to the borders of the Indus at a very early period, if we are to recognise them in the Javana or Jùna and the Dor or Dòdh of the Sanskrit writings, and in the Mùsa and the Lodi of the Musulmans. Be this as it may, however, it seems that these several Greek tribes made numerous and powerful settlements in the territory of our Afghanistan during the period of the Greek sovereignty in that country; for their names, in the forms of Jùna and Yùnus, of Dor, Dorh, and Dòdh, of Aali and Ali, and of Bàe and Bâi, of Mùsa and of Lodì, appear frequently amongst the clans and sections of the existing Afghan tribes; chiefly amongst the Pathan tribes along the Indus border.   Some of these, as the Jùna, Dor, and Bâi have found a place in the Rajpùt genealogies; not as true Kshatrya by descent, but as tribeless Rajpùt by adoption, on account of association and common national interest.   The names Yùnus and Ali are Musulman forms of the Greek Iònoi and Aioloi.   The Greek Akhaioi may possibly in some instances be represented by the Afghan Akà ; but there is a difficulty of etymology here, and it is more likely that the Afghan Akà uniformly represents the Akà tribe of the Nàga, anciently the dominant race in Northern India, and largely figuring in the Sanskrit writings.

Besides the instances above adduced there are some other less known tribes or clans, which may possibly represent the posterity of Greek colonists.   In my " Inquiry " I have briefly adverted to the settlements of his own made by Alexander in the Indus provinces of Afghanistan, as indicated by Strabo ; and in another passage have also noted that, according to Seneca, the Greek language was spoken on the Indus so late as the middle of the first century after Christ ; if, indeed, it did not continue to be the colloquial in some parts of that valley up to a considerably later period still.   Anyhow, from the statement of Seneca, above alluded to, we may conclude that the Greek language was commonly spoken along the Indus, say in the sixth generation, or nearly a hundred and eighty years after the overthrow of the Greek dominion in our Afghanistan by the Jata.   Who, then, were the people by whom this Greek was spoken on the Indus so long a while after the destruction of Greek sway in that region ?   They could be none other than the progeny of the Greek colonists established there some two hundred years before the overthrow of the Greek kingdom of Baktria, above referred to ; a progeny, too, by Greek women, for it is the mother's language which the infant learns.   This is a conclusion which should not excite surprise when we consider the numerous instances, recorded by ancient Greek and Roman writers, of the employment of Greek women in the house-holds of the Indian princes and nobles of that day, and sometimes in the retinue of Greek ladies married to Indian sovereigns and grandees. There is no doubt that the Greeks accompanying Alexander freely took wives from the women of the countries they had conquered ; but after their rule was established under Greek kings, there is equally no doubt that the successive reinforcements they received from the home country were accompanied by more or less large convoys of merchants, mechanics, menials, and emigrants, amongst whom was a no small proportion of Greek women.

Moreover, it is to be borne in mind, that although the Jata deprived the Greeks of the paramount authority and kingly rule, the Greek was by no means thereby effaced, nor at once degraded by the conquest of the barbarian. On the contrary, he long continued to exercise the just influences of his superior knowledge and higher civilization, and probably also, as an honoured subordinate, was granted a fair share in the government and administration of the country from the paramount rule of which he had been deposed. As, indeed, is evidenced by the use of his language on the coinage of the new Sovereigns during several succeeding centuries ; as is attested by the art of his architects and sculptors, the more durable relics of whose work are in our day so plentifully discovered in the ruins of former habitations throughout the area of Greek occupancy in this region ; as is visible in the Greek cast of decorative art, in the domestic furniture and utensils of the people, as practised by them at the present time ; and as is traceable, if I mistake not, in the presence of Greek vocables and derivatives in the very vernacular of the country itself. Results such as these could proceed only from Greeks naturalized to the soil, and maintaining their nationality and civilization, in more or less of integrity, for a long period after their fall from the high position and dominant authority they had possessed and exercised. With the lapse of time, however, and the operation of dynastic changes, the Greeks of Ariana gradually lost their influence through the resulting decay of their national characteristics, and finally—perhaps not before the rise of Islàm—became lost to view in the common multitude of the Infidel of these parts; along with whom they afterwards passed undistinguished into the fold of the Faithful, where we now find their descendants.

The Greeks were dispossessed of Baktria, and deprived of their rule in Afghanistan by the Jata—the Goths of Asia—whose tribes are largely represented in the population of the north-eastern parts of the country, and all along the Indus valley. But before proceeding to notice these later arrivals, we may here conveniently refer to the tribal constituents of the population of ancient Ariana prior to the Alexandrian conquest, or at the period immediately preceding that great event. From the records quoted in our " Inquiry " it appears that the western portion of that region was inhabited by Persian tribes, amongst whom had intruded at a comparatively recent date at that period—the middle of the fifth century before Christ, when Herodotus wrote—various hordes of the nomadic Skythians, called Sàkà, Sakai (Saxons), by the Persians and Greeks respectively.

The Persian tribes mentioned by Herodotus, and stated to have been exempt from the payment of tribute—and probably for the most part inhabiting Persia proper—were the Pasargadai, the Maraphoi, and the Maspioi; the Panthialai, the Derusiai, and the Germanoi, who were all husbandmen; and the Daoi, the Mardoi, the Dropikoi, and the Sagartoi, who were all nomads. These were the principal tribes of the Persians, and they are enumerated by Herodotus in the three separate groups as above distinguished. Of these the first group comprised the tribes of the royal family and ruling classes. Of the three names given, the first in the list and the noblest of all, Pasargadai, is rather a descriptive title than a tribal patronymic. The name seems to be the

Greek form of the Persian *Pisar Kada*—"Sons of the House," which was probably the colloquial term applied to the tribe to which the royal family belonged. In fact, as Herodotus says, "among them (the Pasargadai) is the family of the Akhaimenides from which the kings of Persia are descended." That is to say, one of the Pasargadai, or *Pisar Kada* clans, was called Akhaimenes, which is probably the Greek rendering of a native name—perhaps *Akà-manush*, or "Men of the Akà race"; the Akà being a tribe of the Nàga, to which also belonged the Mada, or Medes. The tribe in which this Akhaimenes, or *Akàmanush*, clan was incorporated, was probably the Kurush (so named after the Kuru, another great tribe of Nàga race), from which Cyrus (Kurush) took his name. The Kurush, as shown by our "Inquiry," are still largely represented by that name in our Afghanistan; of which country itself the Persian king Cyrus was not improbably a native. The Maraphoi may be represented by the *Marùf* sections found in some of the Pathan tribes; the name may also be connected with the *Marùf* district to the south of Ghazni along the western skirt of the Suleman range. The Maspioi may stand for one of the clans of the great Aswa tribe celebrated in the legends of antiquity relating to this part of Asia; the name is most likely the Greek form of *Meh-aspa*, in the colloquial *Meh-Isap*, "the great Isap," and may be now represented by the Isap, Isapzì, or Yusufzì of Afghanistan, the *Aspioi* of Strabo and Arrian.

The three tribes in the second group—Panthialai, Derusiai, and Germanoi—all of whom were husbandmen, evidently represented the settled agricultural or peasant population of the Persian race. The last named is represented now-a-days by the people of the province of Kirman, in the south-east of the modern Persia; but it is probable that formerly a branch of these *Kirmani* had an occupancy on the Indus, where they gave their name to the Kirman district watered by the Kuram river. The Panthialai also, it would seem, formerly had a settlement on the Indus border, for we have a district, in the Mahmand hills north of Peshawar, called Pandiali, which probably took its name from this tribe of the Persians; the Pandiali are not now found as a separate territorial tribe in Afghanistan, though it is probable that traces of them exist among the Tajik population. The Derusiai are now represented in Afghanistan by the Darazi or Darzai tribe inhabiting the Ghor hills to the east of Herat, and supposed to be a branch of the Druses of the Lebanon in Syria.

The third group comprises the four tribes, Daai, Mardoi, Dropikoi (Derbikoi of Strabo), and Sagartoi, all nomades. Each of these tribes is represented in our Afghanistan; the two first named by the Dàhi clans of Hazàrah, among which is one called Dàhi Marda; they are probably more fully represented among the Ilyàt of Persia. The Dropikoi, I have in our " Inquiry " supposed to be represented by the Rajpùt minstrel clan *Dharbi* or *Dharbiki*, from the similarity of the name to the Derbikoi of Strabo; though the Rajpùt are not supposed to have come into these western borders of ancient Ariana at this early period; but they may have been adopted into the Rajpùt genealogies, like many other tribeless clans of Rajpùt. The Sagartoi are not found by that name as a separate tribe in Afghanistan; perhaps they may be included among the Tajik of Sistan, or among the Ilyat of Sagarkand to the south of Sistan; or they may be represented by the Sàgari or Saghri clan of the Khattak on the Indus in Peshawar district.

All the foregoing tribes were of the Persian race proper, and as such exempt from the payment of tribute. Hence their names do not appear among the nations named as composing the several satrapies respectively. Of these last, the tribute-paying nations, Herodotus furnishes us with the names of a considerable number, whose territories lay in the different satrapies or provincial governments which were included within the geographical limits of the ancient Ariana—our Afghanistan—as defined at the outset of our " Inquiry." Almost every one of these nations is to-day represented among the inhabitants of Afghanistan by tribes bearing similar names, and situated in the corresponding satrapies, so far as the position and extent of these are determined by the identity of nomenclature.

For instance, the second satrapy, comprising the Mysoi, the Lydoi, the Lasonoi (called in another passage Kabaloi Meionoi), the Kabaloi, and the Hygennoi, is shown by our "Inquiry" to have occupied that central portion of our Afghanistan which is contained between the Kabul and Helmand rivers on the north and west, and bounded by the Suleman and Khojak Amran ranges of mountains on the east and south respectively. In other words, the second satrapy of Herodotus comprised the modern Afghan districts of Kabul, Ghazni, and Kandahar together. Because the several nations mentioned by him as composing that satrapy are to-day represented in the area above roughly defined by the territorial tribes named Mùsa, Lùdi, Miyàni, Kàbuli, and Khùgàni. The Lasoni are not now found by that name in this area, but they are represented in Balochistan by the Lasi, Lasàni, Lashàri and Laghàri, all variants of the original patronymic Las, after which is named the Las Bèla province of Balochistan. The Lùdi, whose history as an Afghan people is fairly well known, are not now found as a separate territorial tribe in Afghanistan, having bodily emigrated to Hindustan in comparatively recent times. The others are all well-known tribes in the area spoken of.

Again, the seventh satrapy comprised the Sattagydai, the Gandarioi, the Dadikai, and the Aparytai, "joined together," as Herodotus states. Each of these nations I have shown to be now represented by the Khattak, Shattak, or Sattag (for the name is met with in each of these forms), the Gandhari, the Dàdi, and the Afridi; and from their several occupancies along the Indus border, have marked out roughly the situation and extent of this satrapy. It lay along the Indus up to the eastern watershed of the Sulemàn range, and its northern extension of Sufed Koh and Khybar range to the mountains of Bajaur; and extended from the Bolan Pass in the south to the watershed of the lofty mountains separating it from the eleventh satrapy in the north.

The eleventh satrapy comprised the Kaspioi, the Pausikoi, the Pantimathoi, and the Daritai. It lay athwart that just described, through the ancient Paropamisus, from the Arghandab valley in the west to the Kashmir border in the east; being bounded in the south by the second satrapy above mentioned towards the west and by the seventh onwards to the Indus in the east; whilst in the north it was bounded by the twelfth satrapy, to be next noticed. The Kaspioi I have supposed to be a tribe of the modern Kashmir country, and as such beyond the area of our inquiry. The Pausikai I have recognised as the Pàsi or Pàsiki of the Rajataringini, the modern Pashài of Lughman and Ghorband, and in the " Inquiry" have included the Bash or Bashgali of Kafiristan with them, though these last probably derive from a different source; from a later invasion of the northern Nomads, and speaking a different language, though probably of the same stock as the Pasi originally. The Pantimathi I suppose to be represented by the Mati of the Arghandab and Upper Helmand valleys. The Daritai are the Darada of the Sanskrit, the modern Dardu of Dardistan.

The twelfth Satrapy comprised the Baktroi as far as the Aiglai, and is represented by the modern Balkh and Badakhshan, now commonly called Afghan Turkistan. It extends from the Murghàb river on the west to the Sarikol Pamir in the east; being bounded on the north by the Oxus, and on the south by Hindu Kush and Kohi Bàba. It was here that were settled, several generations before the Alexandrian campaign, those Greek exiles from Kyrene and Milesia, the Bàrkai and Brankhai, whose posterity we have recognised in the Baraki and Barangi, at this day dwelling in the very seats originally allotted by Darius Hystaspes and Xerxes to their remote ancestors. And it was here that was established the centre of the Greek dominion in this part of Asia resulting from the conquest of Persia by Alexander the Great. What connection, if any, the one may have had with the other is a very interesting question for investigation by the historian and statesman. For not only have we here the posterity of the Greek exiles above mentioned, but also that of the Greeks who ruled this country as its conquerors and naturalized citizens for a period of two hundred years; from 330 B.C., when Alexander took possession of the country, to 126 B.C., when his successors here were deprived of the government by the barbarian Jata. The Greeks took the country from the Baktri, whom, it would seem, they also deprived of their lands, for the Baktri were the only people who obstinately opposed the progress of Alexander after he had passed from Aria (Herat) into Drangia (Sistan). But however this may be, there are no Baktri now known by that name as a tribe in this satrapy. Their modern representatives are supposed to be the Bakhtyàri (for Bakhtari, from Bakhtar, the native original of the Greek Baktria), now found settled principally in Persia, and scattered about sparsely in different parts of Afghanistan as travelling merchants and carriers ; though they have small settlements in Kandahar, at Margha in Arghasàn, at Dràband in Kolàchi of the Indus Derajàt, and a few other places. In Balkh their place appears to be occupied by the Shekh Ali and Ali Ilahi, or Ali Ali tribes, whom I have supposed to represent the Aioloi Greek; and it is probable that representatives of other Greek tribes may yet be discovered among the so-called Tajik population of the petty States of Badakhshan, inasmuch as many of the existing chiefs and noble families of that country claim descent from Alexander and his followers. In later times a new racial element has been introduced into the population of this province by the invasion of Uzbak and Turkman tribes, mostly nomads; but in numbers sufficient to have acquired for the country the modern designation of Afghan Turkistan.

To the north of this Baktria province, across the Oxus,

and to its west, beyond the Murgàb, lay the sixteenth satrapy of Herodotus, which comprised the Parthoi, Khorasmoi, Sogdoi, and Arioi. Of these nations only the first named and the last come within the range of our inquiry. The Parthoi, who occupied the modern Sarakhs and Mashhad districts, are of interest to us as the nation to which belonged the celebrated Arsaki tribe, now represented by the Harzagi division of the Turkoman of Marv—a tribe anciently associated very intimately with the Greeks of Baktria, and which gave its name to the dynasty more familiarly known as that of the Arsacides. The name Parthoi may be the Greek rendering of the native Pàrs, or Bàrs, which means "Leopard," used as the national designation of the Komàn or Turk Komàn of these parts, according to the usage anciently current amongst the Skythic hordes. In which case the Parthoi of Herodotus would now be represented by the Turkman tribes of the Marv country, who have recently become subjects of the Russian Empire. The Arioi occupied the modern Herat country, and are now represented by the Herati, the Haravi of Muhammadan writers, and perhaps the Haràya of the Rajpùt genealogies. They are not now known as a distinct territorial tribe by that name in the Herat province, but are scattered about in isolated families all over Afghanistan, chiefly in the larger cities and centres of town population, where they are engaged as scribes, shop-keepers, artisans, and so forth.

To the south of the Herat province, the ancient Aria, lay the fourteenth satrapy of Herodotus, which comprised the Sagartoi, the Sarangoi, Thamanai, Utoi, Mykoi, "and those who inhabit the islands on the Red Sea, in which the king settles transported convicts." This satrapy is represented by the modern Sistan province and western Makràn. Of these nations, the Sagartoi have been mentioned above as nomads, and described among the principal Persian tribes who were exempt from tribute. Here we have them again, but included among the nations paying tribute. The

Sarangoi were the same people as the Zarangoi and Drangai, inhabitants of Drangia, the modern Sistan, in which country the site of their capital city is now marked by the ruins of Zarang. The name has been revived in modern times in the national appellation of the Durani, as explained in our "Inquiry," though probably the tribe itself is now represented by the Kàyàni of Sistan, a Persian tribe of ancient date, supposed to be the same as the Kakàya of the Sanskrit writings, and to include the existent Kàkar Pathan of the Suleman range, who are called Kàyan, Kaikàn, and Kaikànàn by Muhammadan authors. The Thamanai are the modern Tymani of Ghor. The Utoi are now represented in Afghanistan by the Utmàn tribes on the Indus border, to which quarter they migrated from the Kandahar country in the fifteenth century as described in our "Inquiry." The Mykoi I have supposed to be represented in Afghanistan by the Màkù, though probably they are better represented in Persia—along with the Uti, also—by the Muki.

The remaining portion of ancient Ariana was covered by the seventeenth satrapy of Herodotus, which comprised the Parikanoi and Asiatic Ethiopians. It lay to the south of the second satrapy, first above mentioned, and is represented by the modern Balochistan. The terms used by Herodotus to designate the natives of this satrapy are somewhat indefinite, though they may be comprehensive enough. The Greek Parikanoi seems to be a close transcript of the Persian form of a Sanskrit designation; of Parikàn, the Persian plural form of the Sanksrit Parva-kà, which means "of the mountains," or "mountaineer"; and may represent the Brahwì of Eastern Balochistan, or the Kalàt Highlands. The Asiatic Ethiopians evidently refers to the various Kùsh, Kash, Kach, Kùj, or Kaj tribes, after whom the country is still named, in its great divisions of Kach Gandava and Kaj Makran. The principal of these tribes was the Gadara, after which people the country was called Gadrosia by the later Greeks. They seem to be the same people as the Garuda (Eagles) of the Sanskrit writings, the inveterate foes and destroyers of the Nàga (Snakes). They are now represented by the Gadari of Las Bèla. Another was the Boledi (mentioned by Ptolemy), and whose real name seems to have been Bola, probably deriving from the Assyrian (Asura of the Mahàbhàrat) Bael, Bal, or Bel. In the foregoing enumeration we have the names of all the principal tribes, as mentioned by Herodotus, inhabiting our Afghanistan in the century preceding its conquest by Alexander the Great. In the Ràmayana, Mahàbhàrat, and other Sanskrit writings, we have the names of many tribes dwelling in these parts at the same early period, some of which are identifiable with nations named by Herodotus, and others of which were probably included among their clans or tribes. But this is too long a subject to enter into now. Nor indeed have I touched it in the course of our "Inquiry"; referring to which I would merely observe here, that among the various names appearing in the sections of the several clans and tribes of Afghanistan, many are recognisable as of Sanskrit record, and as such referable to a period antecedent to the Greek invasion. Thus, from Herodotus on the side of Persia, and the Sanskrit records on the side of India, we are enabled to obtain a fairly complete view of the racial elements composing the population of Ariana at the time of its conquest by Alexander the Great.

By the historians of his campaign, and the geographies of Strabo and Ptolemy relating to this newly-opened part of the world, we are furnished with a different nomenclature of peoples and provinces contained within the region to which our inquiry is directed. Some of these peoples are at once recognised as those mentioned by the earlier authorities above indicated, whilst others are explicitly described as tribes of the invading barbarians by whom the Greek rule and civilization in these parts was overthrown and ultimately destroyed ; but besides these there is a third set of names referable to neither of the preceding categories, and which, though few in number, require further elucidation. The list of these tribes and their allotment in the three categories above mentioned is too lengthy for description here. I merely allude to the subject now, to point out that after investigating all the names of nations and tribes, in this region of Ariana, which are mentioned by the ancient authorities prior and subsequent to the Alexandrian conquest, as above indicated, and adding to these the tribes introduced by the later Turk, Mughal, and Tatar invasions during the Muhammadan period, we still have a few tribal names the affinities of which can be referred neither to the one nor the other of the preceding sources. These tribes, from the similarity of names, I have supposed to represent the posterity of certain Thrakin and Lydian tribes assumed to have accompanied or followed the Greeks, who we know conquered, ruled, and colonized extensively this our Afghanistan some twenty-two centuries ago ; and who, we also now know, established the seat of their authority in the province which for several generations preceding had already been occupied by two distinct and more or less numerous settlements of their own nationality ; and the posterity of which earlier Greek colonists we now discover in the Baraki and Barangi inhabiting the very localities assigned by the ancient authors before cited to the original settlements in this region of the Bàrkai and Brankhai Greeks. Now, if, as seems to be clearly established, the posterity of the Greek exiles above described, first planted in Baktria in the sixth and fifth centuries before Christ respectively, have survived down to our day in the very tracts originally settled by their remote ancestors, surely we may reasonably expect to find some posterity of those Greeks who during the two succeeding centuries at least occupied, if they did not also thoroughly colonize, this same region in vastly greater numbers, and under incomparably more favourable conditions, than were ever enjoyed by their compatriot predecessors above mentioned.

The Afghan tribes which I suppose to be of Greek

ancestry, are the various clans and tribes called Àli or Aàli, representing Aioloi, or Aiolians; the clans and sections called Jùna or Yona, Javana or Yavana by the Hindus, and Yùnus by the Musalmans, representing the Iònoi, or Ionians; the clans called Bàì, Bâè, and Bâìzì, representing the Boiòtioi, or Bœotians, for though in my " Inquiry " I have entered the name as Bâì, dropping the affix -*zì* or -*khel*, as there explained, I should state that the name is invariably, so far as I am aware, met with as Bâìzì, and I cannot cite a single instance of its appearing as *Bâì-khel*, though I know of no reason why it should not so occur also. Besides these names commonly found amongst the clans and sections of most of the Pathan tribes, there are, doubtless, others which have escaped my notice. I have, in my "Inquiry," suggested the connection of the Bàrak, or Bàrakzi, tribe of the Durani Afghan—the tribe of the ruling Bàrakzi Amir of Kabul—with the Baraki above mentioned, the representatives of the Greek Bàrkai or Bàrkæans, of Kyrènè; and should further research establish the reality of such connection, we must reckon the Bàrakzì also as of Greek ancestry, the remotest of all to be found in the country.

Regarding the other tribes, and the origin of the name Afghan, I must refer to the " Inquiry " itself; for my introductory *précis* has already much exceeded the limit at first fixed; and in now concluding my remarks, I would beg it to be understood that my " Inquiry " is what that word signifies, and by no means pretends to a complete elucidation of the ethnography of Afghanistan. The " Inquiry " contains what I have been able to put together in some sort of connected order in the course of a hasty gallop against time over the length and breadth of the wide area of the ancient Ariana, snatching up here and there, wherever recognised, stray relics of the inhabitants of long bygone ages, and tacking them on, wherever they seemed to fit, to those now dwelling in their former occupancies. Such a proceeding on unknown ground would have been venturesome indeed ; but being acquainted more or less with much of the region traversed in our excursion, I venture to hope the results which I have here set forth will not prove altogether profitless, even if they serve no other purpose than to show others where lies a field for most interesting research alike to the ethnologist and the antiquary.

H. W. BELLEW.

20th August, 1891.

Butler & Tanner, The Selwood Printing Works, Frome, and London.

I

THE DIGNITY OF LABOUR, AS TAUGHT IN THE TALMUD.*

"And he said, Ye are idle, ye are idle : therefore ye say, Let us go and do sacrifice to the Lord."—EXOD. v. 17.

NEVER was an accusation more false than this, addressed to the Israelites suffering under Egyptian bondage. They had been building the treasure-cities of Pharaoh, Pithom and Raamses, and had been living a life of toil and labour ; and yet in face of this activity they were accused of idleness and sloth. The charge was as true then as many a one which, at the present day, is levelled at the Jewish people—often for the sole purpose of supplying some grounds for the persecution of this ancient race.

Not unfrequently do we hear it stated against the Jews as a class, that they are averse to manual labour, and shun those walks of life in which work, honest toil, is imperatively demanded.

The highly interesting and candid article in the January number of *The Nineteenth Century*, on "The Jew as a Workman," will do much to dispel many erroneous impressions on this head, as regards the Jew of the present day. But this character of the modern Jew is not a sudden manifestation, it is a gradual growth, the development of a system which found its highest sanctity in work cheerfully undertaken and honestly carried out.

With the Bible as a starting-point, it may not prove uninteresting to trace the growth of this system, to consider briefly what doctrine the Rabbis of the Talmud held upon so important a theme as the duty and nobility of work.

Naturally, they realized that, from the first, work was intended by the Creator as the only means of training and gladdening the human heart, the means of giving man dominion over the earth, and of guarding him against all evil. As soon as man was created he was placed in the

Paper for the **Ninth International Congress of Orientalists,**

London. September. 1801 :   Section (B) 1.

garden of Eden, "to work and to keep it."[1]   Being of a twofold nature, spiritual and material, it was the purpose of his earthly existence that, by subordinating the material to the spiritual endowments of his being, he should perfect himself in the exercise of heavenly attributes; and to ensure this end, the necessity of work was enjoined upon him. This principle was to guard and to guide him—to keep alive and strengthen within his soul the thought of his mission on earth.   It was the only thing which could comfort and rouse him at a time when he failed in that mission and clouded his happy state by sinful action.

"In the sweat of thy face shalt thou eat bread;"[2] it was work alone, honest toil, which in the case of Adam after the fall (as in the case of every son of man) was able to restore him to something of his former state and lost glory.   The doom pronounced by Heaven upon the first man, that he should have to work in order to exist, was therefore less a curse than a blessing.

The passage in the Talmud is most pathetic which tells how, when the words of the curse were pronounced upon Adam, "Thorns and thistles shall the earth bring forth for thee," his eyes began to fill with tears, and he inquired with a bitter lamentation, "Shall then I and my beast share one and the same lot, feeding in one and the same stall?"—whereupon the concluding words of the doom were addressed unto him, "In the sweat of thy face shalt thou eat bread;" and as these accents of Heaven's mercy fell upon his ears, his spirit was revived, he was comforted, and even rejoiced.[3]

The Books of Moses contain no direct reference to work: this was scarcely necessary, considering how deeply rooted this idea of the sanctity of labour was in the human heart. Surely the command to rest on Sabbaths and festivals presupposes engagement in occupation during the week and ordinary days: an idea expressed by the Jewish sages in these words:—"He alone will enjoy the repose of the Sabbath who has laboured on the eve of the Sabbath."[4]

---

[1] Gen. ii. 15.   [2] Gen. iii. 19.   [3] Talmud, Pesachim, 118a.
[4] Talmud, Abod. Sar., 3a.

The whole national life of the Jew, with all its numerous ordinances connected with the soil and agriculture, argued the existence of an active working spirit among the Israelites, and of an industry in all departments of human labour.

Work was both the duty and the blessing of every God-fearing *man*.   As the Psalmist sings : " When thou eatest of the labour of thy hands, happy shalt thou be, and well shall it be with thee." [5]

The " virtuous *woman*, whose price is far above rubies," is she who " worketh willingly with her hands . . . who looketh well to the ways of her household, and eateth not the bread of idleness." [6]

Work it is which, in the words of the Bible, rendereth " the sleep of a man sweet," [7] which " rejoices the heart," [8] by means of which " the hand of the diligent maketh rich, while he becometh poor who dealeth with a slack hand." [9]

How different is the estimate of the value and dignity of labour which we meet in the Jewish code from that which is found in the codes of other ancient systems !   The whole spirit of the Bible breathes the truth epigrammatically expressed in the adage, *Melacha Melucha*, " it is a royal thing to labour," [10] while even among the Greek and Roman nations labour was regarded as the province of the slave— unworthy of the freeborn and noble.

When we contrast, too, the life-teachings of the sages of the Talmud, we shall witness in even a more surprising manner the estimation in which honest toil and manual labour were held among the wisest and best of the sons of Israel.   By their very pursuits they gave practical proof of the sincerity with which they believed that the only method by which man could attain social happiness was by a combination on his part of what they termed *Talmud Torah* and *Derech Erets*, that is, theoretical study and practical pursuits. [11]

A Roman of old would have told with a thrill of pride how Cincinnatus was called from the plough to assume the

---

[5] Ps. cxxviii. 2.   [6] Prov. xxxi.   [7] Eccles. v. 12.   [8] Eccles. ii. 10.
[9] Prov. x. 4.   [10] Commentary on Aboth, *vide Kochbe Jizchak*, xxix.
[11] Talmud, Aboth, ii. 2.

command in the war with the enemy, and how he returned at its close to his former simple habits. Might not the Jew, with equal or greater cause, boast of the simple and industrious habits of the Rabbis of old, who, after discoursing in the college on the most abstruse subjects of learning, betook themselves with cheerful spirits to the occupation which gave them all that they required and desired, namely, " bread to eat and raiment to put on " ?

It would perhaps surprise many, to hear what a variety of occupations was followed by these sages of old. Hillel, the patient Rabbi, we read, was a day-labourer.[12] R. Scheshet was not ashamed to be a wood-carrier.[13] R. Jitschak Napcha was a smith,[14] R. Chanina a pavior,[15] also physician,[15a] R. Jehuda Chaita a tailor,[16] R. Jochanan Hasandler a shoemaker,[17] R. Jehuda Hanechtam a baker,[18] and R. Joseph worked at the mill.[19]

It is a point worth noting, that the Talmud refers to the fact that in Alexandria the number of Jewish artisans and mechanics was so great that they had a large synagogue of their own, in which the members of the various crafts were seated according to their guilds. There were guilds of goldsmiths, silversmiths, braziers, blacksmiths, weavers, etc.[20]

Nor, as is often erroneously supposed, did the Jewish people, and consequently the Rabbis among them, show less willingness in devoting themselves to agricultural pursuits, or display less aptitude in the work of the husbandman. In truth, at one time it was their favourite occupation : pupils and teachers might be seen upon one and the same field, labouring hard in the cultivation of the soil. In this connexion it will suffice to refer to such men as Abaia,[21] R. Asi,[22] R. Samuel,[23] R. Chilkia b. Tobi,[24] Simon of Mizpah,[25] R. Gamliel,[26] and R. Elieser b. Hyrcanus.[27]

---

[12] Talmud, Joma, 35*b*,   [13] Talmud, Gittin, 67*b*.   [14] Talmud, Sabbath, 52*b*.
[15] Talmud, Ketuboth, 112*a*.   [15a] Talmud, Joma, 49*a*.
[16] Talmud, Bab. Bat., 164*b*.   [17] Aboth, iv. 14.
[18] Talmud, Bab. Bat., 132*a*.   [19] Talmud, Gittin, 67*b*.
[20] Talmud, Succah, 51*b*.   [21] Talmud, Chulin, 105*a*.   [22] *Ibid.*
[23] *Ibid.*   [24] Menachoth, 85*b*.   [25] Talmud, Peah, ii. 6.
[26] *Ibid.*   [27] Aboth d. R. Nathan, vi.

None of these greatest of worthies deemed it beneath them to work for their livelihood. No wonder, then, that in the discharge of duty they felt the force of their own dictum, "The day is short, while the work is long."[28] No wonder that they have given to the Jew and to the world at large such priceless, precious sayings bearing upon the blessedness of labour, upon its sanctity, upon its nobility, and hence, upon its obligation upon the sons of men.

The expressions which we meet scattered throughout the length and breadth of the Talmud upon the subject of work, upon the happiness which it confers upon its devotees, could only have emanated from men who had tested their truth by practical, individual experience.

"Love work"[29] was the main idea of the Talmudic doctors; and the scores and hundreds of their more lengthy maxims on the subject are but an amplification and para-phrase of this apothegm.

R. Akiba remarks: God's covenant with us includes the duty of wholesome occupation, for the command which en-joins, "Six days shalt thou labour and do all thy work, while on the seventh day thou shalt rest," made the rest of the Sab-bath day conditional upon our working during the six days.[30]

"And they shall *make* unto Me a sanctuary, and I will dwell among them." The presence of God, adds R. Tar-phon, did not dwell among the Israelites, until they them-selves had with their own hands *made* a sanctuary to the glory of Heaven.[31]

The Rabbis knew of no distinctions of class—no work was considered too menial or degrading, in the attempt to earn an honest livelihood. "Flay a carcase in the market-place, rather than be under the painful necessity of applying for charity, and say not, 'I am of noble origin, I am a descendant of Aaron the high priest; how can I stoop to such an occupation?'"[32]

It matters little, thought the sages, provided the motive be

---

[28] Aboth, ii. 20.   [29] Aboth, i. 10.   [30] Aboth d. R. Nathan, xi.
[31] *Ibid.*   [32] Talmud, Pesachim, 113a.

pure and the means honourable, in what department of human industry we labour. The Rabbinic exegetists, commenting upon the words of Ecclesiastes (iii. 2), "He hath made everything beautiful in his time," remark: "God has so willed it that each man's craft should appear beautiful in his own eyes." [33]

" I am a creature of God, and so is my neighbour. He may prefer to work in the country, I in the city. I rise early to follow one calling, he to follow another. As he does not seek to supplant me, I shall do nothing to injure him ; for I believe that, where the ideal of duty is present before our minds, whether we accomplish much or accomplish little, the Almighty will reward us according to the worthiness of our intentions." [34]

The views of the Rabbis on the importance of the cultivation of land are expressed in sayings such as these :—" He who has no land to till cannot be called a man, for Scripture states : ' The heaven, even the heavens, are the Lord's ; but the earth hath He given to the children of men.' " [35]

" Only when a man cultivates the soil with diligence can he expect to be satisfied with bread : if, however, he neglects the ploughing and sowing and watering thereof, he cannot expect to have his wants satisfied." [36]

There is no excuse for a man however well-to-do passing his days in idleness, for :—" If a man have no other work to do, let him go and attend to the waste fields and dilapidated courtyards which belong to him." [37]

" In the future all trades and occupations shall vanish from off the face of the earth, agriculture shall alone remain." [38]

Not only did the sages of the Talmud dilate upon the sacred character of work in general, but they warned in no equivocal language against the dangers of idleness and the neglect of acquiring some handicraft. It is because they observed and studied the causes of much of the distress and evils of the world that they gave utterance to the

[33] Talmud, Berachoth, 43*b*.
[34] Talmud, Berachoth, 17*a*.
[35] Talmud, Jebamoth, 63*a*.
[36] Talmud, Sanhedrin, 58*b*.
[37] Aboth d. R. Nathan, xi.
[38] Talmud, Jebamoth, 63*a*.

expression : " He is highest in the fear of God who maintains himself by his own labour," [39] while "an inactive life is the very death of men." [40]

R. Elieser says :—" Though a woman may have at her command a hundred servants, she should yet devote herself to some domestic occupation, for indolence leads to vice—R. Simon adding—ay, and to insanity." [41]

" He who does not teach his son some special handicraft, is as though he had trained him to become a robber." [42]

But, on the other hand, " Though the famine may last seven years, it can never reach the door of the industrious mechanic." [43]

Their abhorrence of the doubtful methods of earning a subsistence the Jewish teachers have expressed in these words :—" Happy is the man who has been reared in an honourable calling; woe to the man who has selected a doubtful walk of life !" [44]

While, in their anxiety to prevent pauperism or a recourse to alms, the Rabbis advised their brethren rather to stoop to the most menial pursuit than to beg, they yet offered them the advice that, under ordinary circumstances, in making the choice of a trade, "it was the duty of a parent to have his child taught a trade which was light and cleanly." [45]

" The world cannot exist either without perfumers or without tanners; yet devote yourself to the cleanly work of the former rather than to the unsavoury work of the latter." [46]

It would seem, however, judging from the context, that the sages attached to the expression "cleanly," when applied to work, a deeper meaning than would at first sight appear : that they meant the word to be taken, not so much in the literal as in the moral sense, and standing for "straightforward and respectable." And though a " respectable " calling might not always yield as profitable a return as one of dubious integrity, yet the Rabbis counselled :—" Be it

---

[39] Aboth d. R. Nathan, xi.   [40] *Ibid.*   [41] Talmud, Ketuboth, 59*b*.
[42] Talmud, Kidduschin. 82*b*.   [43] Talmud, Sanhedrin, 29*a*.
[44] Talmud, Kidd., 82*b*   [45] Talmud, Kidd., 82*a*.   [46] *Ibid.*

your ambition to engage in a *clean* pursuit, and leave the issue in the hands of Heaven, prayerfully confiding in Him to whom alone riches and possessions belong; for there is no trade in which fluctuations do not arise, no pursuit in which success and failure do not alternate, and man's good fortune is dependent upon Him who hath declared, 'Mine is the silver and the gold, saith the Lord of Hosts'!"[47]

Instances might be multiplied; but sufficient has perhaps been said to prove how high was the regard for work entertained among the Jews of the Talmudic age. That work itself was looked upon as even a Divine command no one can deny. That it was regarded as a "religious observance" (Mitzvah) in the real sense of the word, is clear, for it was the Rabbis who set down the rule, "He who is occupied with the performance of one religious observance is absolved from the duty of engaging in another;"[48] and it was the Rabbis who absolved those occupied with the handiwork of their craft from engaging in certain duties or submitting themselves to certain restrictions ordinarily in vogue amongst the Hebrews. For example, they excused the labourer from rising—nay, they did not permit him to rise—in the presence of the Sage and the hoary,[49] and from descending from the tree or the waggon or the scaffold[50] in order to repeat so important a portion of the prayer-book as the " Schemang."[51]

This provision had the further effect of ensuring the most scrupulous attention of the employed to the work of the employer. It should be added, that the Rabbis set their face against what is termed " slop" work. Their idea was, that in the long run it paid better to do little work and well, rather than much work and badly. " Take hold of little," say they, " and you have a chance of keeping that little; take hold of much, and you lose all."[52] Or, to cite a maxim derived from horticulture : " Attend diligently

[47] Talmud, Kidduschin, 82*b*.   [48] Talmud, Sotah, 44*b*.
[49] Talmud, Kidd., 33*a*.   [50] Talmud, Berachoth, 16*a*.
[51] The Scriptural passage, Deut. vi , beginning at ver. 4 : " Hear, O Israel,
the Lord our God, the Lord is one."
[52] Talmud, Kidd., 17*a*.

to one garden, and you will dine off birds; undertake the charge of many gardens, and the birds will feed on you." [53]

Not to enter into details, it will also be seen from what has been stated above, that technical education,—a subject which in some countries is only just beginning to receive adequate consideration,—was already a *fait accompli* in the Jewish system of training.

It is remarkable that, amid the devotion which the Talmudists paid to the idea of labour and industry, amid the enthusiasm with which they inculcated this doctrine, both by precept and example—it is remarkable that the difficulties of trade competition should already, so many centuries ago, have been foreseen by them, and its remedies even suggested.

The Mosaic warning, "Thou shalt not remove thy neighbour's landmark," [54] was emphasized by the expounders of the Law, and invested with a meaning which had reference to the workmen of Talmudic times. It admonished them against the guilt of "taking the bread out of one another's mouth;" for, according to the Rabbis, "The man who," in the words of the Psalmist (Ps. xv. 4), "does no evil unto his neighbour," refers to the one who does nothing to damage the chance of his fellow-man's earnings. [55]

The remedy which the Talmudists suggest is, strange to relate, Trade Unionism, which shall make a fair distribution among those willing to work of the labour at disposal, and shall see that while one workman may flourish, another, for want of work, shall not altogether languish and starve. [56]

To show that the spirit of the Rabbinic doctrine on Work —its ennobling character and its obligations—did not depart with the close of the Talmud, but has been carried forward in the life of the Jew to our own days, it may not be inopportune to quote a few words on this point from the Ethical Will of the late Chief Rabbi, which has recently appeared in print [57] : "I need not lay to your hearts the im-

---

[53] Midrasch on Leviticus iii.   [54] Deut. xix. 14.   [55] Talmud, Maccoth, 24*a*.
[56] Talmud, Bab. Bat. 9*a*.   [57] *Vide Jewish Chronicle*, Jan. 9, 1891.

portance of fulfilling your duty during the week, whatever be your calling, by your industry, your unflagging diligence in your employment, whether it be a business or a profession. This diligence must be accompanied by strict integrity, not merely in great, but in the smallest matters, towards your co-religionists as well as to non-Israelites. This integrity will secure to you a good name and the happiness of a calm conscience; but what is of greater value, it will conduce to the sanctification of the Lord and the honour of your faith."

Let those who assert that the teachings of the Jew favour a life of indolence and a shirking of honest labour; let those who cast the slur upon the Jewish people, that, in order that they might lead a life of ease, they are permitted by their Law to prey upon their fellow-citizens—let these open the pages of the Talmud and judge for themselves. There is no necessity, no warranty, for repeating, after thousands of years, to the Jews as a body the unjust reproach of the Egyptian king, " Idlers are ye, idlers . . . go, therefore, now and work." For, hunted and chased as they have been on the high road of time,—their souls well-nigh crushed out by reason of oppression and hate (grim spectres, whose chilling grasp they feel, alas! in many countries still),—there was one ennobling thought ever uppermost in their minds, namely, that though despised, downtrodden, and doomed to indignity of the grossest kind, there remained to them yet the blessing of Work, which, in the words of their sages of old, " conferred dignity upon the worker." [58] Had they lost sight of this truth, they would have been faithless to the covenant of Heaven and to the Holy Law (the Rock to which they clung in their sea of troubles), since it is the opinion of one of the Rabbis of the Talmud that, " The man who does not love work, but shuns work, excludes himself from the covenant with Heaven; for, just as the Holy Law is a sign of the Covenant, so does Work constitute a sign of the Covenant between God and man." [59]

HERMANN GOLLANCZ, M.A.

[58] Talmud, Nedarim, 49b.   [59] Aboth d. R. Nathan, xi.